THE SKY'S THE LIMIT

DON'T GIVE UP

BY SUSANNE M. BUSHMAN

BLUE OWL
BOOKS

TIPS FOR CAREGIVERS

Social and emotional learning (SEL) helps children manage emotions, learn how to feel empathy, create and achieve goals, and make good decisions. Strong lessons and support in SEL will help children establish positive habits in communication, cooperation, and decision-making. By incorporating SEL in early reading, children will be better equipped to build confidence and foster positive peer networks.

BEFORE READING

Talk to the reader about not giving up. Explain that everyone faces challenges.

Discuss: What is hard for you? What do you do when you want to give up? How do you feel when you persevere?

AFTER READING

Talk to the reader about the importance of perseverance and resilience.

Discuss: What would you like to learn or achieve? How can you get there? What can you do to help yourself be resilient in the face of challenges? Who could help you when you feel you need help?

SEL GOAL

Some children may have a fixed mindset. They may not understand that they can develop skills, talents, and abilities by working hard. They may feel that they will never get better at certain tasks or abilities. Help readers develop a growth mindset. Reflect on things that they had a hard time doing at first but can do now. Create a list of things that they would like to work hard on and do in the future.

TABLE OF CONTENTS

CHAPTER 1

WORK HARD

Everyone has talents. Maybe you are good at soccer. Or maybe reading comes easily to you.

But not all tasks or skills are easy. You might struggle with math. You want to stop trying. It would be easier. But don't give up!

Trying hard is a big part
of learning and growing.
It is important for you to
be the best you can be!
You are an important
part of your community.
You can make a big
difference in the world!

STRONG BRAINS

Every time you work hard
at something, your mind
gets stronger! **Neurons** in
your brain form stronger
connections. You get smarter!

CHAPTER 2

FACE CHALLENGES

Not giving up requires work. Sometimes this means being **patient**. Maybe the fish aren't biting. You ask to quit. But you and your grandpa stay. You finally catch one! It was a fun day.

Patience helps you do long projects, too. Maybe you're doing a puzzle. It's hard to find pieces that fit together. But you keep looking and finish it. It is **rewarding**!

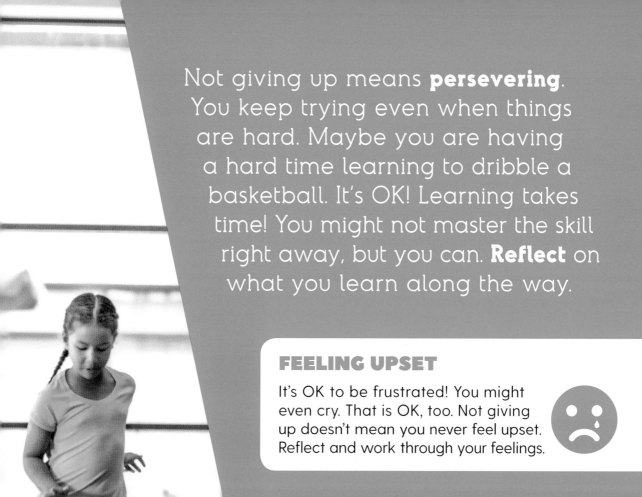

Not giving up means **persevering**. You keep trying even when things are hard. Maybe you are having a hard time learning to dribble a basketball. It's OK! Learning takes time! You might not master the skill right away, but you can. **Reflect** on what you learn along the way.

FEELING UPSET

It's OK to be frustrated! You might even cry. That is OK, too. Not giving up doesn't mean you never feel upset. Reflect and work through your feelings.

Maybe you dream of being an actor. But that dream seems far away. Don't give up. Show **grit**. How? **Focus** on your passion. Set **goals**. Practice your lines for the school play every day.

THINK BEFORE YOU QUIT

Sometimes, you might want to quit an activity. But think before you do. Don't quit on a hard day. It may just be a **setback**.

Be **resilient**. Maybe there are bullies at school. Or maybe you have lost someone you love. Don't let these things stop you. Keep doing your best.

ASK FOR HELP

Everyone has a hard time sometimes. But if you are struggling for a long time, talk to an adult you trust. Nothing is too bad to talk about. Asking for help doesn't mean you gave up.

CHAPTER 3

BUILD STRENGTH

Make never giving up a **habit**! How? Try focusing on the steps instead of the results. Maybe you are trying to put together a toy. But it isn't working. Try again! Finding the answer can be part of the fun.

Changing your **mindset** can make it easier to not give up. Maybe you're having a hard time focusing. Try to be **mindful**. Focus on the present. What are you trying to do?

Turn to your **network** when you want to give up. They can **encourage** you. You can help them, too! Cheer on your friend at her soccer game. Help your classmate. Hug your mom after she had a bad day.

When you don't give up, you can do amazing things! You can finish projects. You can gain new skills. You can achieve goals. You can grow up to have a cool job.

CONFIDENCE IS KEY

Make a list of things you are good at. Spend time doing them. Trying hard is easier when you feel **confident**!

GOALS AND TOOLS

GROW WITH GOALS

Not giving up can be hard! But it gets easier with practice, reflection, and help from our networks.

Goal: Reflect on your strengths. What are you already good at? What makes you feel confident? Were you always good at those things? How have you improved those skills with hard work?

Goal: Identify your goals. What is one thing that you want that you'll need to work hard to achieve? Write it down! Create a collage that helps inspire you to meet your goal.

Goal: Find a role model! Do you know of someone who doesn't give up? Or you can do research to find someone from history who didn't give up. Use that person as a role model when you're thinking of giving up.

WRITING REFLECTION

Feeling good about yourself helps you not give up! Reflecting on good qualities helps us remember that we can be successful and resilient.

1. What are your favorite things about yourself?

2. What have you done recently that made you proud of yourself?

3. Write about a time when you didn't give up or were successful despite hardship.

GLOSSARY

confident
Having a strong belief in your own abilities.

encourage
To give someone confidence, usually by using praise and support.

focus
To concentrate on something.

goals
Things that you aim to do.

grit
Passion for and perseverance toward very long-term goals.

habit
An activity or behavior that you do regularly, often without thinking about it.

mindful
A mentality achieved by focusing on the present moment and calmly recognizing and accepting your feelings, thoughts, and sensations.

mindset
Mental attitude.

network
An interconnected group of people.

neurons
Cells that carry information between the brain and other parts of the body.

patient
Able to put up with problems or delays without getting angry or upset.

persevering
Continuing to do or try something, even if you have difficulties.

reflect
To think carefully or seriously about something.

resilient
Tending to recover easily from misfortune or change.

rewarding
Offering or bringing satisfaction.

setback
A problem that delays you or keeps you from making progress.

TO LEARN MORE

Finding more information is as easy as 1, 2, 3.

FACT SURFER

1. Go to www.factsurfer.com

2. Enter "**don'tgiveup**" into the search box.

3. Choose your cover to see a list of websites.

INDEX

Blue Owl Books are published by Jump!, 5357 Penn Avenue South, Minneapolis, MN 55419, www.jumplibrary.com

Copyright © 2020 Jump! International copyright reserved in all countries. No part of this book may be reproduced in any form without written permission from the publisher.

Library of Congress Cataloging-in-Publication Data is available at www.loc.gov or upon request from the publisher.

ISBN: 978-1-64527-202-1 (hardcover)
ISBN: 978-1-64527-203-8 (paperback)
ISBN: 978-1-64527-204-5 (ebook)

Editor: Jenna Trnka
Designer: Molly Ballanger

Photo Credits: s_oleg/Shutterstock, cover; oleg66/iStock, 1; LightField Studios/Shutterstock, 3; kdshutterman/Shutterstock, 4, 5; Hill Street Studios/Getty, 6–7; XiXinXing/iStock, 8; BestPhotoPlus/Shutterstock, 9; FatCamera/iStock, 10–11; vgajic/iStock, 12–13; Steve Debenport/iStock, 14–15; chinahbzyg/Shutterstock, 16; kali9/iStock, 17; fizkes/Shutterstock, 18–19; Jose Luis Pelaez Inc/Getty, 20–21.

Printed in the United States of America at Corporate Graphics in North Mankato, Minnesota.